ADVERTISING

Mark McArthur-Christie

OXFORD
UNIVERSITY PRESS

For Nick Cook, who wrote the book before me.

OXFORD
UNIVERSITY PRESS

Great Clarendon Street, Oxford OX2 6DP

Oxford University Press is a department of the University of Oxford.
It furthers the University's objective of excellence in research, scholarship,
and education by publishing worldwide in

Oxford New York

Auckland Bangkok Buenos Aires Cape Town Chennai
Dar es Salaam Delhi Hong Kong Istanbul Karachi Kolkata
Kuala Lumpur Madrid Melbourne Mexico City Mumbai
Nairobi São Paulo Shanghai Taipei Tokyo Toronto

Oxford is a registered trade mark of Oxford University Press
in the UK and in certain other countries

Published in the United Kingdom by Oxford University Press

Text © Mark McArthur-Christie 2002

British Library Cataloguing in Publication Data

Data available

ISBN 0 19 917443 1

10 9 8 7 6 5 4 3 2

Also available in packs
Communications Mixed Pack (one of each book) ISBN 0 19 917446 6
Communications Class Pack (six of each book) ISBN 0 19 917447 4

www.oup.com/uk/primary

Printed in China

Acknowledgements

The Publisher would like to thank the following for permission to reproduce photographs:
p 4 Mark Mason Studios (right); p 6 Ancient Art & Architecture (all); p 8 Robert Opie Collection (left),
Hulton Getty (right); p 9 Hulton Getty (left); p 11 Domino Printing (top), TP Activity Toys Ltd., (bottom);
p 12 Bodleian Library (top); p 13 Hulton Getty (left); p 17 Marin Bikes (right); p 18 Robert Opie (all); p 19
Robert Opie (centre & bottom right), John Frost (top right); p 22 Hulton Getty (top); p 23 Walkers Crisps
(top), Henkel Consumer Adhesives (centre); p 24 Ancient Art & Architecture (top), LCI Adidas (bottom);
p 25 Ben & Jerry's Ice cream (top right); p 29 GreenNet; p 30 Shout Picture Agency (centre right).

Additional photography OUP ©

Front cover photograph by Science & Society Picture Library
Back Cover by Robert Opie Collection

Illustrated by Chris Brown, John Holder and Stefan Chabluk

Despite every effort to trace copyright holders, this has not been possible in every case.
If notified, the publisher will be pleased to rectify any omissions at the earliest opportunity.

The views expressed in the advertisements used as examples in this book are not those
of the Author or the Publishers.

CONTENTS

ADVERTISING IS EVERYWHERE!

Look at the advertisements all around you. Outdoors, you will see posters on shop windows, bus shelters and by the roadside, all advertising something. Open a newspaper or magazine and you will find advertisements. You can hear them on the radio, see them on the television and even play with them on the Internet. Can you see **logos** on the clothes someone is wearing? These are advertisements too, showing the name of the company that made them.

See page 20

▲ You could put your own advert in a shop window.

Adverts can be ▶ written down, like this advert in a newspaper.

▼ This person is giving away free samples – this is advertising too.

▲ Adverts can be expensive. Last year, one company in the UK spent £24 million on advertising their products.

Every day you will see hundreds of them – but what *is* an advertisement?

> An advertisement is a public message that tries to persuade you to buy something or to do something.

Advertisements are often called "adverts", or just "ads".

An advert can be small and cheap; you might write a card and put it in your newsagent's window to sell your bike or find customers for your car-washing business.

You might think that advertising is a modern invention: in fact, advertising has been around for over 2000 years, as these timelines show.

This book will show you about how advertising began and how it has changed.

OLD ADVERTS TO NEW – From the Ancient World to the 21st century

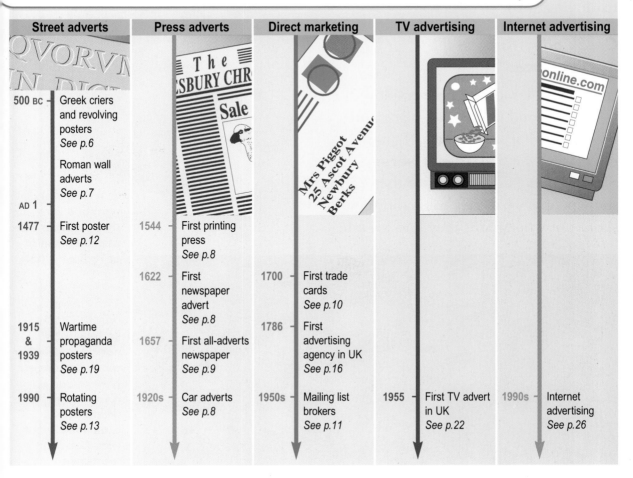

Street adverts		Press adverts		Direct marketing		TV advertising		Internet advertising	
500 BC	Greek criers and revolving posters See p.6								
	Roman wall adverts See p.7								
AD 1									
1477	First poster See p.12	1544	First printing press See p.8						
		1622	First newspaper advert See p.8	1700	First trade cards See p.10				
1915 & 1939	Wartime propaganda posters See p.19	1657	First all-adverts newspaper See p.9	1786	First advertising agency in UK See p.16				
1990	Rotating posters See p.13	1920s	Car adverts See p.8	1950s	Mailing list brokers See p.11	1955	First TV advert in UK See p.22	1990s	Internet advertising See p.26

5

WHERE ADVERTISING BEGAN

Until about 500 BC most people in the Ancient World lived in small groups, growing crops and hunting enough food to feed their own families. Around 500 BC some of these groups began to gather together and live in towns and cities. This meant people could meet to exchange goods. They might have traded spare food for a new axe or a pot. Soon people in cities began advertising the spare things they had made or grown.

Greek advertising in the market place

In Greek cities, criers were employed to walk around the market place and shout out what was for sale. These criers were the first **advertisers**. Shopkeepers had signs above their shops to show people what they sold, and they would shout out what goods they had for sale.

▲ A Roman shop sign for a wine shop found in the ruined Roman city of Pompei in Italy

◄ In Greek cities, notices to advertise sports and games were put up on revolving pillars where people could read about their favourite sportsmen.

How the Romans advertised

By AD 400 the Roman Empire had conquered most of the known world, and the Romans traded with many different countries. In every city there were lots of Roman merchants buying and selling, so they had to advertise to stand out from each other.

The writing on the wall

Roman shopkeepers paid people to go out at night and write big signs on the sides of buildings and at the public baths where everyone gathered.

Traders who had travelled to distant parts of the Roman Empire often had a lot of goods to sell, so they paid a man to shout out what they had on offer.

When the Roman Empire came to an end in the 5th century AD, the towns the Romans built became deserted. People went back to living in small groups where they only grew just enough food for their families. There was nothing to spare, so there was no need to advertise.

▲ These signwriters were called *scriptores* and had helpers called *adstantes*, who held their ladders, and *lanternari*, who held flaming torches.

READ ALL ABOUT IT!

Advertising in newspapers

If you open a newspaper today it will be packed with advertisements. There are lots of different types of adverts, from big companies selling their products, to "small ads" put in by people wanting to sell things they do not need any more. National papers are read by hundreds of thousands of people, and even local papers are read by thousands. When newspaper advertising started, things were very different…

ADVERTISEMENT FOR
SUNBEAM · CARS

The output of Sunbeam Cars is controlled so that each car may be turned out as perfect as picked materials and supreme workmanship can make it. That is why it is still a distinction to drive a Sunbeam.

★

THE SUPREME SUNBEAM. The 25 h.p. Limousine, a seven-seater enclosed car on six-cylinder chassis, provides a brilliant example of coachwork. The superbly built body with all its rich equipment costs you but £455, for while the price of the chassis is £795 that of the complete car is only £1250. Dunlop tyres standard on all models—19 h.p. to 35 h.p.

THE SUNBEAM MOTOR CAR COMPANY LIMITED, MOORFIELD WORKS, WOLVERHAMPTON
LONDON SHOWROOMS AND EXPORT DEPARTMENT: 12 PRINCES STREET, HANOVER SQUARE, W.1

▲ This is an old magazine advert from the 1920s, advertising new cars.

BAGGY KNEES AVOIDED
BY USING THE
"UNITED SERVICE" TROUSERS STRETCHER
PATENTED
IN ALL
COUNTRIES.

FROM ANY TAILOR,
or post-free for 3s. 9d., 5s. 6d., or 6s. 6d., from the
PATENTEES AND SOLE MANUFACTURERS,
Green, Cadbury, & Co., Birmingham.

▲ Papers printed adverts for all sorts of different products. Here is an advert for a machine that stops trousers going baggy at the knees.

The first newspapers were handwritten newsletters, so only a small number could be copied and given out. It was only after the printing press was invented in 1544 that hundreds of copies of a newspaper could be printed. This would have been a good place to advertise, but the first "press advertisements" only began to appear in 1622. Advertisers were slow to see how easily newspapers could get their message to a lot of people.

When new, faster printing presses were made in the 19th century, newspaper owners needed to make more money to pay for this new machinery. They earned money not just by selling the papers, but also by charging the advertisers. So they began printing even more advertisements in the papers. Soon whole pages were covered with adverts.

▲ This modern magazine just has adverts for lots of different things for sale, or "wanted". It does not contain any news or articles. The first all-adverts newspaper appeared in 1657.

Modern advertising in newspapers is a very specialized business. There are companies that just buy space in papers for their clients; other companies specialize in writing and drawing the adverts. Advertising in newspapers today is very different from those old handwritten newsletters!

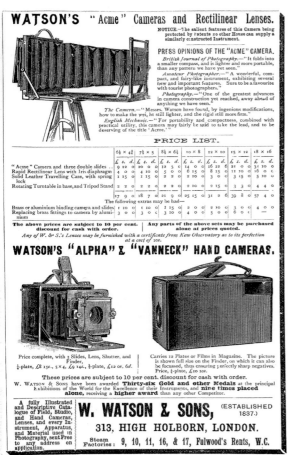

◄ This advert is for cameras. Because it was difficult to print pictures, most old adverts had a lot of words instead. Look in a magazine and compare this old advert with one for a modern camera.

9

SELLING DIRECT

How Direct Marketing began

Newspaper adverts are read by many thousands of people but only a few of those people will want to buy the things being advertised. By sending adverts directly to the people who are likely to want to buy a particular product, the advertiser can save money. This is called **direct marketing**.

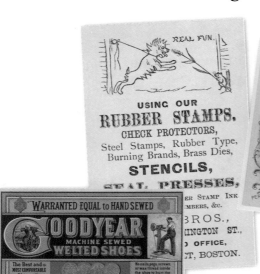

◄ Direct marketing started in the 1700s when tradesmen pushed advertising cards through the doors of rich people's houses. By the 1860s tradesmen were using eye-catching designs to advertise their goods.

There was a postal system in Britain from the mid 1600s, but sending letters was often slow and expensive, depending on where you lived. However, after the introduction of the Uniform Penny Post service in 1840, postmen would deliver letters anywhere in the country for the cost of a penny stamp. This made it easier to send adverts for a product directly to people who might buy it.

How direct marketing works today

To help advertisers to make sure their adverts go to people who want to buy, companies called "list brokers" were set up in the 1950s. They have lists of the names and addresses of people who may want to buy certain products. The list brokers sell these **mailing lists** to advertisers. The advertiser writes an advertising letter and a leaflet and sends it to the right people on the list.

People fill in coupons on the leaflets, or from a paper or magazine, and send them back to the advertiser, either to order a product, or to ask for more information.

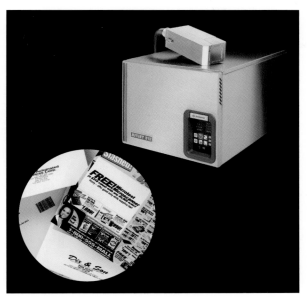

▲ Because the letters can be printed and put in envelopes automatically, by special machines, advertisers can reach a lot of people at one time. This machine can print more than 1000 envelopes an hour.

▲ The art director and copywriter in an advertising studio, working together on the design of an advertising leaflet

This **mailpack** is advertising activity toys. ▶ Because each sheet only costs a few pence to print, companies can afford to advertise their product to a lot of people.

11

POSTERS

Posters are one of the oldest ways to advertise. The first posters were painted or scratched directly onto walls by the Greeks and Romans, but later they were printed on paper and stuck to buildings.

See page 7

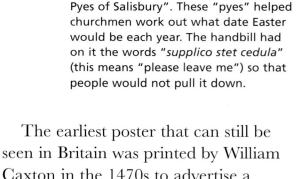

▲ Caxton's first advertising poster, "The Pyes of Salisbury". These "pyes" helped churchmen work out what date Easter would be each year. The handbill had on it the words *supplico stet cedula* (this means "please leave me") so that people would not pull it down.

The earliest poster that can still be seen in Britain was printed by William Caxton in the 1470s to advertise a religious book.

As towns and cities grew, it was important for advertisers to get their message to as many people as possible, so more and more posters were printed and stuck on walls. Until 1855 posters were cheaper than advertising in the papers because newspaper advertising involved paying **taxes**.

Newspaper advertisements were taxed according to size, so they were usually small and were often easy to miss. Posters were tax-free, so they could be

▲ Some posters were painted directly on walls, and you can still see some of them on old buildings today.

▲ Some businesses asked famous artists to draw pictures for them, like this poster advertising a play in Paris.

▼ These posters rotate so that people can see two or three adverts in the space one would normally fill. Adverts like these are very expensive!

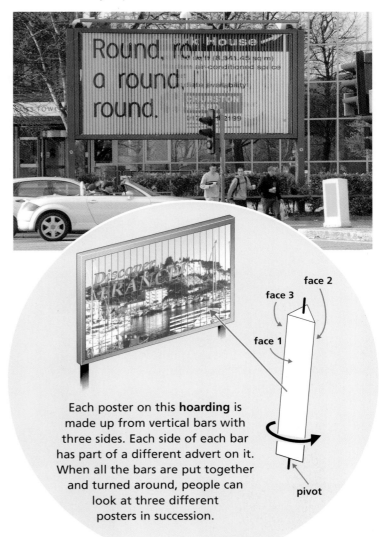

Each poster on this **hoarding** is made up from vertical bars with three sides. Each side of each bar has part of a different advert on it. When all the bars are put together and turned around, people can look at three different posters in succession.

big and eye-catching, with large pictures. Advertisers could print them quickly and send them out to be "posted up" within a day.

Because posters were cheap, more and more were printed and stuck to walls. Then more were stuck on top!

Soon, companies began to buy the right to stick their posters in certain places. They could also **rent** the space to other companies for a fee. Today, a small number of firms own nearly all the poster sites in the UK. They make a lot of money by renting them to advertisers.

THE POWER OF THE PACKET

Bringing adverts home

Advertising on packaging began a long time ago. About 3300 years ago, wine jars from Canaan, in the Middle East, were stamped with the date the wine was made, whether it tasted sweet or dry, the type of grape it was made from and where the grapes were grown.

Packaging keeps what is inside safe, but is also a powerful way for advertisers to make sure people keep seeing the company name whenever they open their cupboards. Every time you reach for a sauce bottle you will recognize it by its packaging and see the advertiser's name.

Most of the things you can see on this ▶ sauce bottle label work like symbols that tell a more complex story.

The label looks old-fashioned because the makers want to give the impression that the sauce is carefully made in a traditional way.

The picture of the Queen's coat of arms is called a Royal Warrant. It shows that the product is of such good quality that it is used by the Queen's household.

The printed signature on the bottle shows that this is genuine Worcestershire sauce. At one time, the makers would actually sign the label to show that it was really made by them. The label also uses the words "The original and genuine" for the same reason.

What was there before packaging?

Groceries used to be sold from big bins in shops. The shopkeeper would weigh out the amount the customer asked for and wrap it up in plain paper. In the 1930s ready-packed groceries became more common. With the arrival of self-service supermarkets in Britain in the 1960s, the companies that made the groceries had to make sure their packages stood out from other **brands** on the shelves, so they designed packets that would attract a buyer's attention.

Look in a supermarket the next time you go shopping and see how many different packages for one product you can see.

▲ There are dozens of different kinds of cereal. Each company tries to make their packages "stand out" from the others.

HOW ADVERTISEMENTS ARE WRITTEN

The first advertising **agency** in England was started in 1786 by William Tayler. It employed just a few people. Modern agencies can employ many hundreds of staff who write and draw adverts for the **clients**, book time on television or space in newspapers and on **hoardings**, and make sure the client's advertising goes out on time.

Who's who in the Agency?

▲ An *account manager* deals with clients, passes their instructions on to the team of people who actually create the adverts, and organizes the printing and production.

▲ An *art director* designs the advert and makes sure it is clear to read or watch.

◀ A *copywriter* writes the words used in an advert, and often comes up with the ideas behind the *advertising campaign*.

How do adverts work?

These two adverts, one from 1900 the other from 2001, both work in exactly the same way. They both show the best things about the products they are selling.

The proposition: This sums up why you should buy the product in a simple message.

A picture: This shows buyers what the product looks like or how easy it is to use.

Copy: This explains the good points about the product and tells you what it does.

Contact details: This tells you where to buy the product or get more information.

17

Dos and don'ts

There are lots of messages the Government wants people to listen to, often about health or road safety. They put up posters and run advertisements on TV.

▲ This advert tries to make people more careful about coughing and sneezing, which spreads germs.

▲ This advert reminds people to use lights on their bicycles at night.

▲ The British Government controls cigarette advertising by making tobacco companies put "Health Warnings" on cigarette packets and advertisements. These are meant to discourage people from smoking by telling them about the dangerous effects of tobacco. The Government does not allow posters advertising cigarettes to be put up close to schools.

Advertising in wartime – propaganda

Sometimes, during a war, a Government wants to tell people that the war is going better than it really is. They get the newspapers to publish stories that make some battles seem like great victories, even if they were not! This is called **propaganda**.

This is one of the ▶ most famous advertising posters. It shows General Kitchener, a British general who led troops in the First World War. He is appealing to people's loyal feelings by telling them that their country needs them to join the army and fight.

HAIG'S NEW BLOW.

GREAT BATTLE FOR CAMBRAI.

A SURPRISE FOR THE GERMANS.

ITALY STEADY.

FRESH ADVANCE IN PALESTINE.

The War : 4th Year : 111th Day.

The Hindenburg Line has been smashed by the Third British Army under General Byng on a front of 10 miles between Arras and St. Quentin. Our troops have advanced four to five miles, and by last night were within three miles of Cambrai.

This blow on the Western front

▲ This battle was reported as a great victory, but was really a disaster. Many men died and there was only a small advance.

This advert appealed to people's feelings ▶ of loyalty during the Second World War. It reminded people not to talk about things that might help the enemy. Humour was used to show that the enemy might be listening! People remembered the jokes and the "catchy" messages, and repeated them to each other.

WHAT IS A LOGO?

Most companies **register** their logos as **trademarks**. This means that no one is allowed to copy them, by law.

a

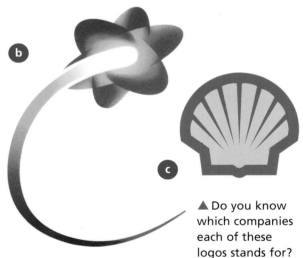

b

c

▲ Do you know which companies each of these logos stands for?

(*See Answers on page 32*)

▼ Logos often try to tell us something good about the thing we are buying. This logo from 1901 tries to show that the biscuits inside the box will be fresh.

NABISCO

FACT BOX

A **logo** is a picture that represents a company or what it makes.

Almost everything on the supermarket shelves has a logo. Logos are usually simple so they are easy to identify. They help people to recognize products and **brands** quickly.

▼ Sometimes, packages themselves are like logos. You know just what is inside this Jif lemon squeezer, the jar with "a piece of chocolate" on top, and the enormous "mint with a hole".

◀ Logos can be used for other messages. The "litter logo" shows someone dropping litter in a waste bin. Look for it on crisp bags and sweet packets.

▲ The Kellogg's logo started out as a hand-written label on cereal packets, over 70 years ago. It still looks a little like handwriting today.

See Answers on page 32

▼ Look at these modern logos – can you guess what products they are for?

TELEVISION ADVERTISING

Say it in 30 seconds

TV advertising is one of the most powerful types of advertising. It combines moving pictures, speech, music and special effects which allow advertisers to put across complicated messages quickly and easily, and repeat them often. As TV **airtime** often costs thousands of pounds a minute, speed is very important!

▲ The first TV advert in Britain was seen on the evening of Thursday 22 September 1955 (when TV pictures were still only seen in black and white). It was a 60-second advert for Gibbs SR toothpaste, and was followed, in the same break, by an advert for Cadbury's drinking chocolate.

Why advertise on TV?

TV is the most efficient way to reach millions of buyers. By choosing the intervals during the most popular programmes to advertise in, companies can make sure their adverts are seen by as many people as possible. But airtime at these **peak viewing times** is very expensive.

Look and listen out for these features in TV adverts:

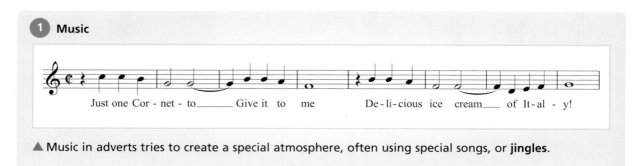

1 Music

Just one Cor - net - to_____ Give it to me   De - li - cious ice cream_____ of It - al - y!

▲ Music in adverts tries to create a special atmosphere, often using special songs, or **jingles**.

2 Characters

◄ Some adverts show the same characters with the product in different situations, turning the advert into a short "soap" story. Sometimes famous people are used to make products seem more appealing. This advert uses Gary Lineker to advertise crisps.

3 Packshots

◄ Most adverts show pictures of the product. This advert sold wallpaper paste in a new way! This huge poster was hung from a crane.

4 Endlines

◄ The endline is part of the voice-over. It sums up the advert.

ADVERTS ALL AROUND US

One of the oldest adverts is the shop sign, showing what is on sale inside the shop. In London in the Middle Ages, there were so many shop signs that some people thought they blocked out the sunlight! Many people could not read or write but they learnt to recognize the signs and so knew what goods or services a shop sold.

Different ways to advertise

Advertisers have always looked for clever, eye-catching ways to advertise. In Ancient Greece, some people had nails on the bottoms of their sandals so that they printed an advertising message in the sand as they walked.

See page 6

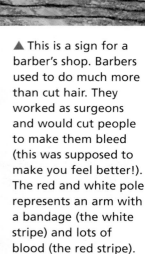

▲ This is a sign for a barber's shop. Barbers used to do much more than cut hair. They worked as surgeons and would cut people to make them bleed (this was supposed to make you feel better!). The red and white pole represents an arm with a bandage (the white stripe) and lots of blood (the red stripe).

▲ This advert for trainers used a giant slide projector to show a picture of these three footballers on the white cliffs of Dover.

These adverts for ice ▶ cream were printed on special coats worn by cows! They were known as "cowverts". Some adverts were printed on the shells of eggs. They were called "eggverts".

▲ Mobile advertising posters can often be seen on buses. Some adverts are difficult to understand. What do you think this one means?

◀ Advertisers get people to try their products by giving away free samples. They hope the people will like the product and buy it from the shops.

ADVERTISING on the WORLD WIDE WEB

Using the Internet, or World Wide Web, is one of the newest ways of advertising. Website addresses are appearing everywhere. It is an important and powerful way to advertise because so many people now use computers every day. It is much easier and quicker to change a page on a website than it is to print an advert or send out a direct mail pack.

The Internet combines ordinary advertising methods in a new way. Web **browsers** can control what they look at by choosing which pages to view, so advertisers have to make their adverts very interesting and exciting!

Cookies

Sometimes web pages have games to try and keep you looking at the site. Many companies can record which pages you look at on their website by using **cookies**. These electronic trackers can remember who you are, and what you like, when you come back to the site, and then bring up the pages they think you will want to see.

▼ Website images can combine words, sounds, pictures and movement.

- moving pictures, sound and spoken words

- written words

- still pictures and pictures in 3D

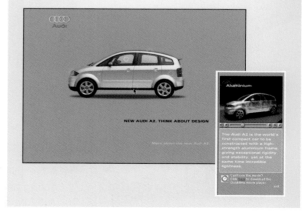

26

The three types of advert on the Internet

1 "Banners" try to encourage you to click on them and visit the advertiser's website. They often have moving pictures to attract your attention.

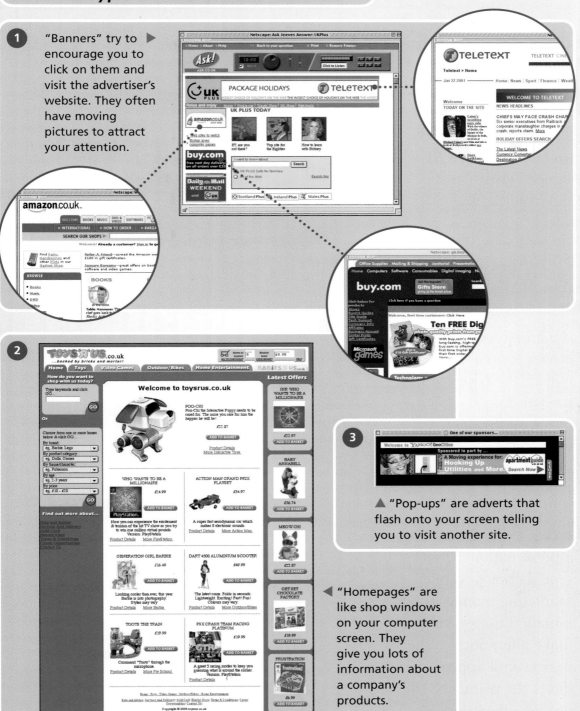

2

3 ▲ "Pop-ups" are adverts that flash onto your screen telling you to visit another site.

◀ "Homepages" are like shop windows on your computer screen. They give you lots of information about a company's products.

ADVERTISING... PAST AND PRESENT

In the studio

In the past, creating the adverts, publicity material and packaging for a product involved a whole team of copywriters, designers, artists, photographers and printers.

Many companies today use computer-aided design (CAD) which enables a single person to

- design packaging or an advert for a product
- choose the typeface for the wording
- check all the details, such as the exact size
- import scans of photographs or drawings.
- create a storyboard for a presentation
- send a copy to the marketing managers by e-mail, for approval
- make alterations to the design until approved
- direct the printer to produce the number of copies required.

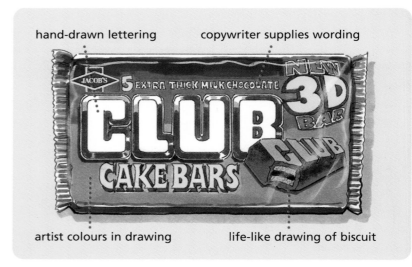

hand-drawn lettering   copywriter supplies wording

artist colours in drawing   life-like drawing of biscuit

▲ The design for this product was created by hand on a drawing board. If anyone wants to change anything, the artist has to draw it all over again.

Design option 1

Design option 2

Design option 3

Design option 4

Design option 5 – chosen design

◀ This product design was produced using CAD.

Advertising overload

Today, there is more advertising than ever before. Some people think there is too much. They arrange to have their names taken off **mailing lists**, and use special video recorders that record just the TV programmes, and not the adverts.

With special equipment, it is also possible to select only the types of adverts you want to see on TV. One person might only be interested in cars and food, for example, but prefer not to waste time watching adverts for beauty products or pet food. Another person might choose just the opposite.

Advertising makes some people angry. They think that it can make people greedy. Others think that companies should not spend lots of money on advertising when it could be used to help people in need.

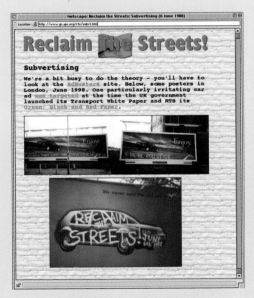
29

ADVERTISING... THE FUTURE

Advertisers are always looking for new ways to persuade people to buy their products. Sometimes they use an old type of advert with a clever new twist. Or they might use a tune or song that was once very popular, but link it with a brand new product. The music will bring back happy memories for many people and make them feel good... and this will encourage them to buy the product.

When you **log on** to the Internet, you will see banner adverts trying to grab your attention by flashing or moving. If you are interested, you can visit their **websites** by clicking on each banner. Not only will the advert that comes on the screen tell you all about the product, you will probably be able to order and pay for it immediately, **online**.

With a WAP ▶ phone you can view adverts and order goods immediately.

▼ On the Internet, if you like the look of a banner advert you can visit its website, if not, you can just ignore it.

See page 27

If you have Direct Response Television (DRTV) you can order goods just by pressing a button on your TV remote control.

On some mobile phones, called WAP phones (Wireless Applied Protocol), you can see adverts on the screen and order the product there and then.

Advertisers have been coming up with new and different ideas since ancient times. They haven't run out of ideas yet, and there are plenty more on the way!

▲ With DRTV you can order a hot pizza and have it delivered to your door!

GLOSSARY

advertisers Companies or individuals who work in advertising.

agency A company that makes adverts.

airtime The total length of time that an advert is shown on TV.

brand A wide range of goods sold by one company under a particular trade mark.

browsers Computer software that lets people look at webpages.

client The person or business who pays for advertising.

cookies Computer software that "remembers" which parts of a website someone has looked at.

direct marketing Selling by post.

hoarding A roadside board displaying an advert.

jingle An advertising slogan set to music.

log on Start to use the Internet.

logo Picture or symbol that represents a particular company.

mailing list A list of names and addresses to which sales letters and adverts can be sent.

mailpack A package of letters and adverts sent to everyone on a mailing list.

peak viewing times The times of day when most people are watching TV.

propaganda Government advertising.

register To put something on an official list of names.

rent Money paid to use something, but not own it.

subvert A way of changing an advert to make it say the opposite of what the advertiser intended

taxes Money that people and companies have to pay to the government.

trademark A company's registered name or emblem, used to distinguish it from other companies or their products.

website A company's place on the Internet which acts like a shop window.

INDEX